Awesome Animal Adventure!

Pauline Cartwright

Contents

Awesome Animal Adventure

Hi there! My name is Dr Dig and I think animals are **awesome**. I love them all – the big and the small.

I'm going to take you on an awesome adventure through time. We're going to learn about some of the biggest animals that ever lived. We're even going to see the **biggest** animal of all time! Can you guess what it is?

Giants of the Past

If we really want to find out about giant animals, we have to go way, way back – to the time of the dinosaurs. Dinosaurs lived between 230 and 65 million years ago. Some dinosaurs were small, but many **species** of dinosaur were among the largest animals that ever lived.

Argentinosaurus

Argentinosaurus

The biggest dinosaur we know of was the Argentinosaurus. Argentinosaurus lived about 95 million years ago. It was a long dinosaur – even longer than a basketball court. Argentinosaurus bones were found in Argentina, in South America. So it was named after this country.

Argentinosaurus	
Size:	35 m long
Weight:	90 tonnes
Diet:	plants
Lifespan:	may have been 50–100 years

Sauropods

Argentinosaurus was a sauropod. There were many different kinds of sauropods, but they all ate plants. They had very long necks and long tails. Sauropods were the largest animals ever to live on land.

Barosaurus was also a sauropod.

Argentinosaurus was the biggest animal ever to walk on Earth! But it's not the biggest animal of all time. Sounds tricky, eh? Keep reading …

Crack the Whip!

Sauropods had long, long tails. Some sauropods may have cracked their tails like whips. This would have made a sound like thunder! This would scare away any likely **predators**.

This is just one part of an Argentinosaurus's backbone!

Spinosaurus

The largest meat-eating dinosaur we know of was Spinosaurus. Spinosaurus lived about 119–93.5 million years ago. Its back spines were the size of a tall man! These spines may have been covered with skin – just like a sail on a boat.

EXTINCT

Spinosaurus

Size:	18 m long
Weight:	9 tonnes
Diet:	meat
Lifespan:	about 40 years

Scary!

The spiny "sail" on Spinosaurus might have scared away attackers. It made Spinosaurus look even bigger than it already was!

I don't think I would like to go sailing with a Spinosaurus!

Tyrannosaurus Rex

Tyrannosaurus rex is one of the most famous dinosaurs. It may not have been the biggest, but it was still a giant.

Tyrannosaurus rex lived 68–65 million years ago. T. rex looked fierce, but it may not have been a great hunter. Some scientists believe that it may have been a **scavenger**, eating animals that were already dead. It's impossible to know for sure!

What's in a Name?

Tyrannosaurus rex's name means, "tyrant lizard king". "Big scary lizard" would suit it, too!

EXTINCT
Tyrannosaurus Rex
Size: 13 m long
Weight: 7 tonnes
Diet: meat
Lifespan: about 30 years

The End of the Dinosaurs

The last of the dinosaurs died about 65 million years ago. Scientists believe that an **asteroid** may have crashed into Earth. This would have caused lots of dust and clouds to block out the sun for many years. Without warmth and light, the dinosaurs couldn't survive.

But that didn't mean the end of giant animals.

Mammoth Mammals!

After the dinosaurs died, more and more species of mammals **evolved**. Most of these mammals were small, but many were enormous.

The woolly rhinoceros could grow up to 2 m tall with a 1 m long front horn.

Giant Rhinoceros

You've probably seen pictures of a rhinoceros. Maybe you've even seen one at a zoo? They're pretty big, aren't they? But scientists have found a **fossil** of an enormous rhinoceros that lived 25 million years ago.

This giant rhinoceros doesn't look much like the rhino we know today. For a start, it doesn't have any horns on its nose. And that long neck looks like it belongs on a giraffe!

a modern-day rhinoceros

EXTINCT

Giant Rhinoceros

Size:	5.5 m tall at shoulder
Weight:	10–20 tonnes
Diet:	plants
Lifespan:	unknown

Woolly Mammoth

The woolly mammoth is a cousin of the elephant. The woolly mammoth lived during the **Ice Age**, a time of **extreme** cold, ice and darkness. It had a thick coat of fur, which would have come in handy.

Woolly mammoths weren't much bigger than elephants, but they were still huge! Their tusks were longer and more curved than those of the elephant. Woolly mammoths may have used their tusks to push ice and snow out of their way to find food underneath.

Dressed for Winter

The woolly mammoth's thick fur coat was made up of a double layer of hair. Below that was a very thick layer of fat.

EXTINCT

Woolly Mammoth

Size:	4–5 m tall at shoulder
Weight:	8 tonnes
Diet:	plants
Lifespan:	about 60–80 years

Woolly mammoths became **extinct** around 9000 years ago. So how do we know about them? Scientists have found whole woolly mammoths frozen in ice. The ice **preserves** the body, often for thousands of years. Some woolly mammoth bodies have been so well preserved that we can still see their fur and eyelashes.

This is Dima, a baby woolly mammoth. She was frozen in ice for 40000 years!

In Search of Food

Like elephants today, woolly mammoths travelled in herds. They roamed the land eating grasses, flowers and leaves.

Giant Ground Sloth

The word "sloth" means slow, or lazy. Sloths today really live up to their name! They spend most of their time hanging from trees and only move when they have to.

But during the Ice Age, sloths were very different. These animals were huge – even bigger than an elephant. In fact, they were about the size of a woolly mammoth. They were too big to hang from a tree, so they walked on the ground instead.

Giant Ground sloths ate plants. They had big claws on their front legs, which they used to pull branches from tall trees.

Walking Tall

The Giant Ground sloth spent a lot of time walking on two feet, a bit like a bear. Just imagine – an animal bigger than an elephant walking on two legs!

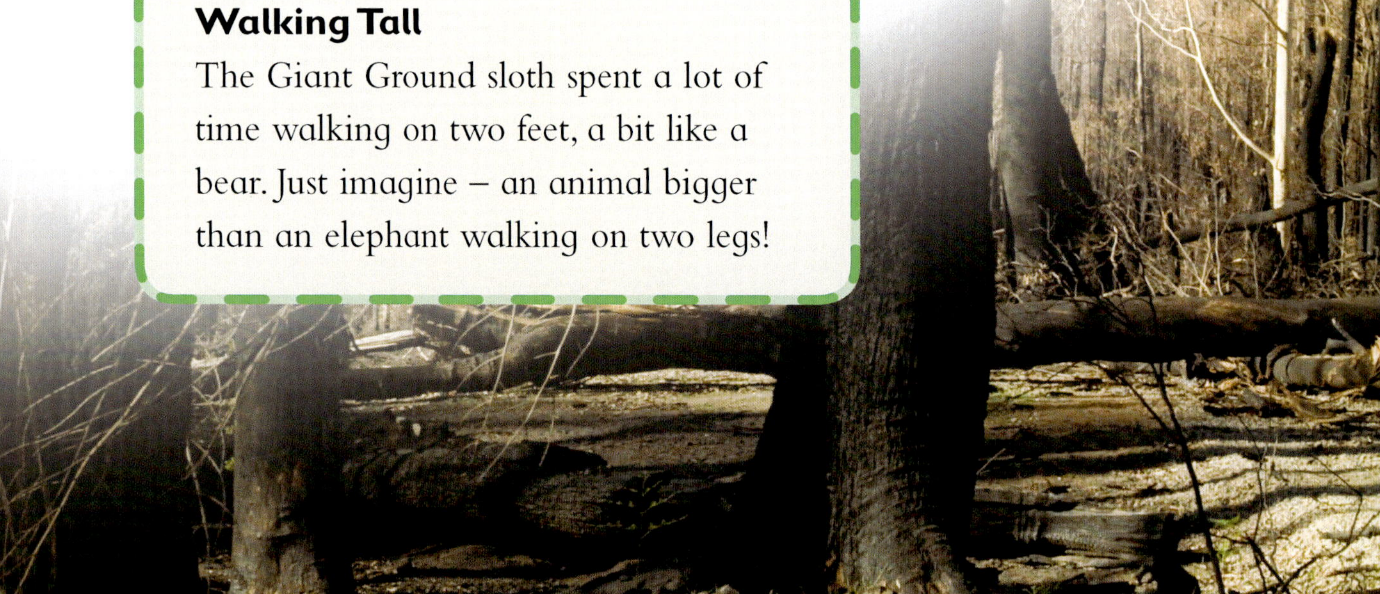

EXTINCT
Giant Ground Sloth
Size: 6 m long
Weight: 3.8 tonnes
Diet: plants
Lifespan: unknown
Next stop – the present day!

Giants Among Us

Here we are, back in the present day. There are plenty of giants left for us to see – including the biggest animal of all time! But let's take a look at these other giants first.

The African Elephant

We've heard a lot about elephants already on our tour. We've even met their ancient cousins. So let's find out more about this giant of our own world.

There are two types of elephant, African and Asian. The African elephant is the larger of the two. It is the biggest land animal today.

ALIVE

African Elephant

Size:	3–4 m tall at shoulder
Weight:	3–6 tonnes
Diet:	plants
Lifespan:	about 70 years

What's the Difference?

African elephants have much bigger ears than Asian elephants. They have a dip in their back, and their tusks are usually larger than Asian elephants' tusks.

Colossal Squid

The Colossal squid is one of the largest animals in the ocean. It has a large reddish-pink body, with arms and **tentacles** about 2 metres long.

The Colossal squid has sharp hooks at the ends of its arms and along its tentacles. These hooks have been known to cause serious injuries to whales that like to eat this squid!

All the Better to See You With!

The Colossal squid has eyes that are as big as basketballs. They are the biggest eyes of any known animal.

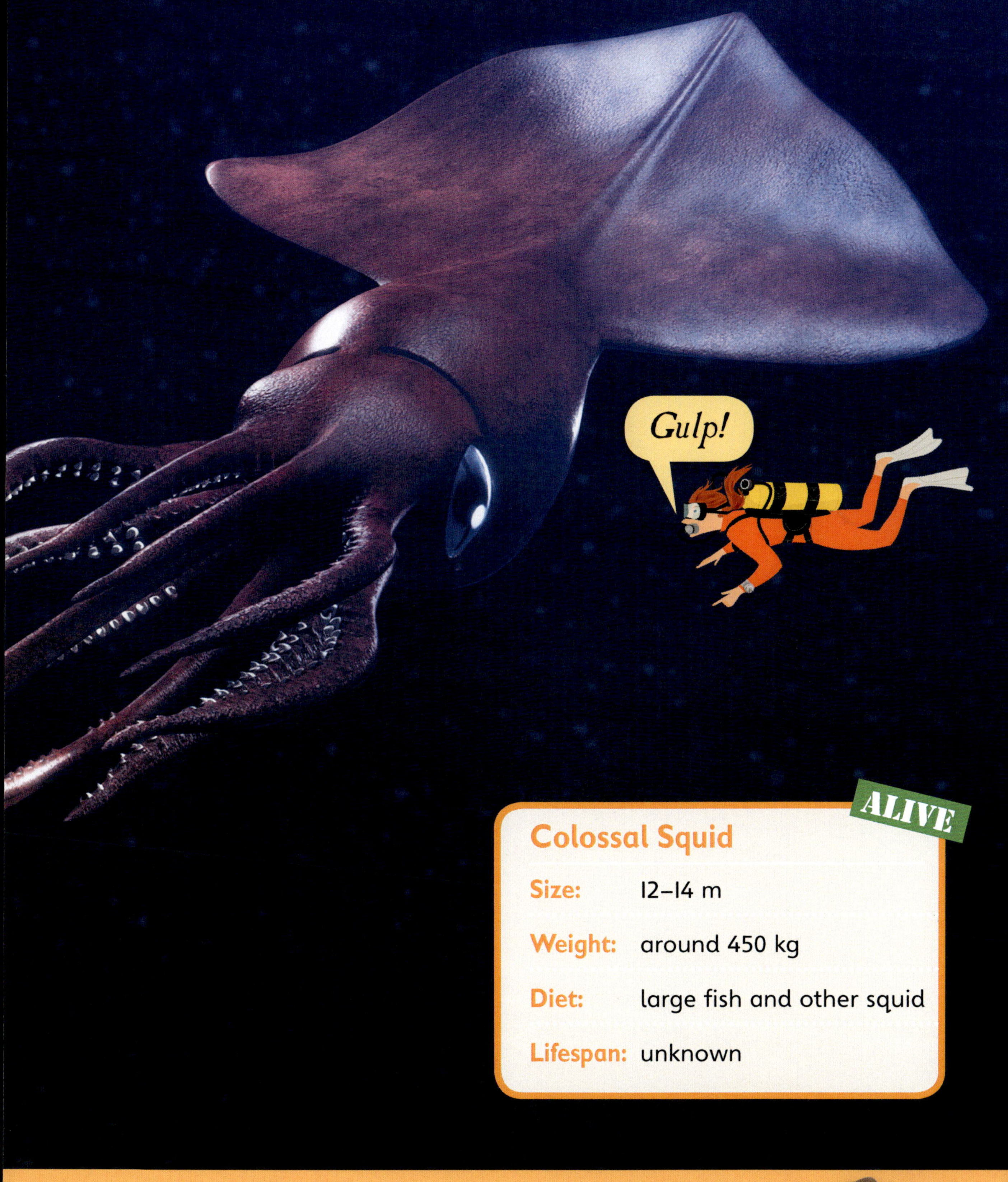

Colossal Squid

Size: 12–14 m

Weight: around 450 kg

Diet: large fish and other squid

Lifespan: unknown

The Biggest Ever!

Here we are, at the end of our tour. And we've kept the biggest till last. The elephant may be the biggest animal that lives on land today, but the biggest animal on Earth lives... in the ocean. It's the blue whale.

The Blue Whale

The blue whale is not just the biggest animal alive today – it's the biggest animal that has ever lived!

That's right. It's even bigger than Argentinosaurus. The blue whale's tongue alone weighs as much as a small elephant!

A newborn whale is 8 metres long.

Blue Whale

Size: 33 m long

Weight: up to 180 tonnes

Diet: krill and other small marine animals

Lifespan: around 85 years

Big Appetite, Tiny Food!

The blue whale may be the biggest animal, but its favourite food is one of the smallest. Krill are very tiny shrimps about the size of a jellybean! A hungry blue whale can eat 3 tonnes of krill a day, which is about the same weight as 6 cows!

Coming Up for Air

Whales are mammals, not fish. They can't breathe under water. They can dive to 500 metres, but must come up to the surface to breathe. The blue whale can stay under water for about 30 minutes.

Blue whales have **baleen plates** on their upper jaw instead of teeth. The baleen plates are a kind of **filter** made of the same stuff as your fingernails. The whale gulps a mouthful of seawater then pushes it back out through the baleen. All the krill and other small creatures get left behind for the whale to swallow.

Just Imagine...

Many of the animals we've seen today are extinct. But think how the world might look if they were still alive. Imagine sharing our streets with a woolly mammoth, or a Giant Ground sloth! It's probably just as well we're never likely to meet Spinosaurus or Tyrannosaurus rex... but it's still fun to imagine a world in which they're still alive!

That truly would be awesome!

Well, that's it – the end of our tour! I hope you've enjoyed it as much as I have.

Glossary

awesome
amazing, wonderful

asteroid
a piece of rock or metal, in space, that moves around the sun

baleen plates
bony but springy plates that hang from a whale's jaw

evolved
changed slowly over time

extinct
when a species of plant or animal dies out

extreme
to a high degree

filter
something used to stop small particles mixing with air or water

fossil
remains of a plant or animal that lived a long time ago

Ice Age
a time in the past when much of Earth was covered in ice and snow

mammals
warm-blooded animals that produce milk for their young

predators
animals that hunt and eat other animals

preserves
keeps in good condition

scavenger
an animal that feeds on dead animals

species
a group of animals that are alike

tentacles
long, flexible body parts used for gripping